LIFE
LINES

POETRY FOR YOUR SOUL

LAURA DI FRANCO

Life Lines
Poetry For Your Soul
©Copyright 2025 Laura Di Franco
Published by Brave Healer Productions
Cover design by Dino Marino
Cover art by Jezhawk Designs
Interior design by K.J. Kaschula

Paperback ISBN: 978-1-961493-74-2
eBook ISBN: 978-1-961493-75-9

LIFE LINES

POETRY FOR YOUR SOUL

LAURA DI FRANCO

Contents

May hope and wonder keep you alive.
May joy and love help you thrive.
May purpose fuel your drive.
May you find your kind.
May you realize
you belong.
And when you don't, grab a life line.

These words are in celebration of my younger self at about 15. Thank you for grabbing your journal and pen when nothing else made sense. I love you.

Introduction

Sometimes, the difference between life and death is one line.

Life lines sometimes glow bright like green neon signs. And sometimes, they seem to hide and it feels like searching for buried treasure you were never given a map for.

But *you* have control over whether or not they glow.

The difference is a subtle shift in awareness from mind to body.

Let's be bodyful.

You can do it now in one, deep, pelvic bowl breath. Feel the movement of your inhale as the ribs expand in all directions. Sigh on the out-breath. Soften.

Body awareness allows you to notice the messages moving through you, understand the language of your soul (the language of your intuition and higher self), and then choose (with clarity) what'll bring you the most joy, love, or anything else you want for your life, maybe even just the will to live. Coming back down into your body is the first step to authentic healing.

You are the one with the answers.

It's time to learn to use your superpowers.

Any single line in this book could change your life—"life lines."

How do they make you feel?

Read them.

Inhale.

Exhale.

Write them.

With awareness, you have a choice. Choose love.

Poetry is one way I live in full expression of who I am. My words, lines, phrases, and pages aren't meant to have to be analyzed. They're meant to guide me (and you) to the light and love I am (you are).

There have been so many times when one line changed my perception and awareness, and in doing so, changed my life.

Think of it. You were going along merrily thinking and living a certain way, and BAM, from the next moment later, everything changes, and you're not only thinking and believing something different, you've changed your habits and behaviors that are the very things creating your life.

Your life changes - in one line.

Life lines. Written or spoken, what power they have if we're paying attention!

Look for the brave spaces in your life. . .

. . . breathe, and choose love.

You are the answer.

When you come up against yourself, again
what will you say?

When you hear the call of your soul,
will you answer or hide?

When you dream your biggest life alive
will you open your shaman heart and let it in?

When you arrive fully in every magic moment and know
will you believe?

And when you finally believe in yourself, in it all,
will you go for the love you are without looking back?

Will you play for the rest of your days
sharing who you were born to be?

You are who you've been waiting for.

From the heart without fear

Dear reader,

Grab your pen and use the prompt pages, even if it's a few words, to move what's in your heart to the page. Write to shift the energy. Write to heal.

With warrior love,

Laura

A Battle Cry

a little girl
screaming in silence
the vibrations stick
and reverberate
against my heart walls
ping off my soul
dent my worth

inhibited forever
small as a habit
told I should
and made to believe
I navigate
in a much wiser body now
question things a lot

a grown woman
screaming in silence
the vibrations rip
and tear
until I pry open a path
for release
and paint it with courage

a warrior goddess
perfecting my battle cry
the vibrations soar
and spread
from my gut to the sky
from my heart to the world
from my soul to yours.

From the heart without fear

Your turn. Let your words out. What do you feel?

What You Survived

Do you sometimes wonder
if what you survived
is a test?

Like, what doesn't kill me
makes me stronger
kind of F'd up lesson-test
to see just what you're made of?

And you do survive it
looking back with a combo side-eye,
eye roll
I'm not sure if that was a cosmic joke
or I should be stoked
kind of look.

And you move on
move forward
take the next steps
think positively in the right, best direction
resting in the closure
proud of the soul you've become as a result. . .

. . .only to wake another day
to a slap in the face
standing there stunned
looking up,
like, "WTF. . .
. . .I thought I'd been tested enough,
thought I'd been there done that,
thought you'd wrung out
every last drop of my capacity
to cope on that last round."

And your mind catches fire again
when you realize
it's never the final round
until you're dead.
But for a moment you stop
and think about the score
and smile.

You're standing in the ring.
You're telling the story.
The opponent may look a little bigger this time
but the reality is
you've won every round.

EVERY SINGLE ROUND.

You lived to tell the tale
to help someone else
to take the experience
and teach
and speak
and love
and be. . .
. . .exactly who you are
as a result of your ability
to stand back up
after being knocked to the ground,
and ground yourself in the deep exhale of purpose.

YESSS. . .
YOU did that!

Congratulations, you survived.
And you will again.
And if you're wondering,
you're not alone.
Everyone's in that ring
even if you can't see it.
Everyone is struggling to stand back up again.
And there's no rule we can't offer a hand.

Let's go warrior.
You got this next round
no matter what's thrown your way.
Training is never easy
but it's what gives you the power
to do this life with grace and ease
and a touch of badassery.

"And. . . in this corner, ladies and gentlemen,
we have reigning world champion
of the realities of life, never give up until you die,
throw a bucket on the fire of your mind
and choose a better fight, survivor. . . (Fill in your name).

From the heart without fear

Your turn. You survived. Now what?

Brave Spaces

I feel brave spaces
between the hush of my breath
and the midnight stars
stuck in that sweet knot in my throat
as inspiration shifts it a bit
and it slides from my heart to my tongue
and begins to sound like a song
written about your smile.

Dark hours hold some
before dawn
before the first bird song
before I commit
to fully living that day.
I pray for more light:
"Please, illuminate my why
no matter what the naysayers say."

I catch one like a firefly
carefully cupping it to my face
peeking at the glow
hoping for a trace of magic
something to show me
I'm meant for this world
that I belong
that my voice matters
that you see my heart.

I start finding parts in the pain
in the center of the rocks
harder as the clock ticks
knowing about the treasure
like geodes
If, oh gee, only I'm brave enough
patient enough
strong enough
to dig deeper

wake from the sleep
notice the weight of five decades of shoulds
piled on my soul plate.
Brave spaces rest in those layers
where curiosity is gold
and I'm sold on peeling them away one by one
until I'm free
can breathe
feel like me again.

Nowadays, all I need to do
is gaze at the sunrise sky
notice the still points in my life
between slower in and exhales
the choice between fear and love
the pause of my pen
before the next line
the rhyme in line nine.

I realize brave spaces
are everywhere we stop
drop into the present of the moment
get under the fire of our mind
to find "Will they like me?"
and spin a different tune to the mirror.
"Hey, love warrior, I see you. Come and play!
Saving the world works better
when you love yourself first today."

Where are the brave spaces in your life?
Hiding in plain sight.
Cowering in old stories of blame
energy lodged in your gut
a web of shame setting the table to feed
off the chaos, mess, and uncertainty
banking on your inability
to just be and feel.

And there it is again my friends,
Brave Healers. . .
. . .you know how to feel.
You've connected to the most mind-blowing
magic in all the land.
Put your hand on your heart
sink in for a while.
Let the Divine soul that is you
take the wheel.

Open her up
on a road you haven't traveled
as much.
Feel the wind in the stillness,
the excitement and purpose in your fear.
Instead of riding the brake
using anxiety as the fuel in your tank
trust and squeeze the gas pedal
get a little Thelma and Louise on life's ass.

It's always good to remind yourself
at the end of this ride
the goal isn't getting out alive.
Dive into every brave space in your life
your heart, your mind, and your alien soul
like never before.
Dance, sing, play, paint, and write
through the pain
and especially the joy.

Brave is so much better
when joy shouts, "Shotgun!"
and the two as one, take the darkness on.
Each space, each step,
each curve of your words lights the path.
Keep going until breathing syncs up
the lines of truth start to blur
and the sound between your sigh and the stars
is, "I love you."

From the heart without fear

Your turn. Where are the brave spaces in your life?

A Smooth Ride to Paradise

It was a smooth ride to paradise
Caribbean breezes
remind me to soften
while I can
A mini-lifetime begins
the moment I notice

Be happy
Be sad
I'm okay with flowing forth and back
in the unknowing
the let-go-ing
I embrace the life in my tears
as heartily as the smiles
content in the sweet fullness
of the gift
however it looks or fits expectations

I face each many end
with ease
see purpose in change
turn the page after the last word
hold disappointment gently
until lines blur
and death starts to seem
like a part of life to be curious about
instead of dread

And then. . .
. . .I'm taking another smooth ride to paradise

From the heart without fear

Your turn. Take a moment to feel. What do you notice?

Perfectly Broken

Sometimes the ache is so bad
you can't breathe.
Hours disappear
and you don't remember
how you got from there
to here
and you'd swear
the death grip in your chest
will be the end.

One more second.
One more gasp.
You even gently wait for it.
But that's the thought
that opens you up
cracks the window
lets in the breeze.
An inhale so big
it breaks your soul free
to cry
to be
broken
perfectly.

Simultaneously
the grip eases
helping you realize
it's not here to stay
but to help you train,
condition your heart,
strengthen that part always worried
it can't carry the weight of the world
one more day.

Follow the ache
to the breath
to the thought
to the ease
to the strength
to the knowing.

Your heart will carry all the sorrow
and all the joy
without bursting
without busting
without exploding
or ripping apart.

But sometimes this starts
with an ache so bad
you're convinced
everything you've built
will all come crashing down
when really
it's just about to get good.

And what you can do
is remember to believe
breathe
feel
and be
perfectly
broken.

From the heart without fear

Your turn. What if the broken parts created your superpower?
What is it?

Lemon Perfect

Worry follows from a dream
into the crisp dawn
squeezing at my chest and throat.

What do snakes mean?
Does he really have to die?

I remember to get wise.

What meaning makes sense to you?

I'm busy shaking fear off my
sweaty skin
picking scabs of lingering dread

Inhale
followed by full-body release.

It's in your head.

I'm back on the path
morning bird symphony
like confetti in my ears
a rainbow of spring greens
making pinks pop like fireworks
the gentle backward tug of the
leash
slowing me down
so I won't miss a scent.

My sense is knocked back in
teasing thin strands at first
then all at once
like my soul cannon-balling
into my heart pool.

Oh, that's better, I think.
I'm back.
Here is where it's at.

Like a gulp of Lemon Perfect
sliding down my dry throat
I'm quenched.

Heaven sent this day to me.
I will not miss it.

Drink up.

From the heart without fear

Your turn. What dreams follow you into your day?

Awakening

This fear isn't mine.

I looked seven generations behind.
The lightbulb blinded me.
Confusion disappeared.
The very straight line pointed to me.

Fear was stuck
thick-crusted and glued to my heart.
I pried away pieces for years
pulling off huge chunks of flesh
to save myself from the pain.

I discovered octopus powers.
Something brand new grew
whenever the sharks dismembered me.

All I needed was time to heal
awareness to feel
wisdom to recognize the deal
I made with God.
And I knew.

I'll be the one to alchemize the fear
into fuel.
I'll be the one to clear the line.
I'll be the one who alters time.

I floated and breathed.
I noticed crow's wings
illuminated gold on sunrise beams.
I stared into a circle of rainbow spears
shimmering in the sky.

I touched my third eye
and remembered to listen—closely.

It's time to be brave.

From the heart without fear

Your turn. What doesn't feel like yours?

Girl On the Moon

I love the snow
that slips in quietly overnight
gifting my morning (and life)
with a pause.

An abundance so great
there's no question:
You aren't going anywhere
for a while.

A blanket so white
it brightens the pitch-dark
without the moon.

A layer so soft and fresh
it drops a playground
all around me.
I hear the invitation,
"Can you come out and play?"
like the other end of the phone
in grade school.

The parka goes over the sweater
pulled over the dry-fit T,
puffy hat, waterproof gloves
Lands End boots, one by one.

I crack the door just an inch
at first
smell the burst of winter sky
watch so many tiny flying things
dig for the seed I left yesterday.

Good timing, I think.
Blinking my watering eyes
I set out
minding the first step with the ice
and leaving the first footprints
like a girl on the moon.

From the heart without fear

Your turn. What makes you feel like a kid again?

What's Done is Done

Good morning, sweet child
child of the sun
What's done is done.
Who are you today?

Sing your song
Dance your dance
Show us the magnificence
that is your soul

Beyond all you've been told
Beyond all fear controls
Beyond the wounds
mothers and grandmothers couldn't unfold

Touch the place inside
The fire in your heart
Show and tell the wild desire parts
It's your turn; you're up next!

Remember to keep your eyes up
locked with your healer friends
when you test your courage again
Grab hands!

Good morning, sweet child
child of the sun
What's done is done
Who are you TODAY?!

From the heart without fear

Your turn. Write about one of your wild desires.

The Only Goal

Everything I want is already mine
I breathe peace
thick and sweet
like morning in July
A deep sigh
melts the 30-year clench
My soul settles into morning songs
My hum joins the harmony
I wonder
Do they hear me, too
when I bask on the patio
in my cushioned blue lounge?
Can I tune my heartstrings well enough
to win a chair in this world-class symphony?
I notice more perching above
Yes, it's possible
It may be the only goal worth striving for.

From the heart without fear

Your turn. Listen with your heart. What do you hear?

Rest

Rest
Let the soft, solid earth
cushion each step
Sweeten each breath
in spring greens
Connect to the gentle beat
in your chest
syncing to the rhythm
of what pulls you deeper.

Let the mountain water
rush through your worries
Let them ride on tiny wings
and blend into the joy song
DJ-ing the sunrise
Surprise your soul
with how long you can
sit still in it.

Bask there
perched in the wonder of life and death
soaring for a higher perspective
Let this freshness
help you come alive
Remember the child inside
who only ever wants
to laugh and sing and dance in the breeze.

Pause in the field of wishes
and make everyone
as if they're already done
Watch as the sun beams magic
over the trees, turning them gold
like you're the only soul
she's performing her show for
because right now, you are.

Rest your heart
your mind
your alien soul
Be kind to yourself
Allow it *all* to heal you
Open with a breath
Deep and wide is best
Nothing to do but be.

Rest.

From the heart without fear

Your turn. Can you allow the present moment to heal you?

One Breath Away

I claim healing today. . .
. . . knowing I'm enough
with every scar and failure,
every stupid choice I later regretted.

How else can I wake up
to enjoy the miracle of tomorrow
to feel grateful
to be love to give love?

I'll slow down when I can
but I embrace each quick start
fueled by Divine inspiration.
I trust those moments now.

I've mastered the language.
It's only a remembering away.
I know the big-M me.
I learned to listen.

These aren't risks
they're investments in purpose.
It's so simple.
Why wad it into excuses?

It's never complicated.
It's joy or not.
It's love or not.
It's light and free or not.

I love the contrast for teaching me,
the tightness for helping me notice,
the weight and darkness of the no
for being obvious and too much to hold.

It's clear.
Experiences may feel complicated
but there's discernment and mastery
in the pulse of alignment.

It's easy to feel what is
when you stop trying to make it
what you think you want
and just let it be what it is.

What if it was all meant for you?

What if it's all a miracle?

What if you're only one breath away from love?

From the heart without fear

Your turn. What do you forgive yourself for?

The Shawl

The slow, heavy, damp
of an uninspired day
week
month
wraps itself around my shoulders
like an oversized shawl
and keeps me warm.

The cozy weight
reminds me
there is good in here
that still, slow pace
nothing to do
nothing to be
much to feel.

Turning off the tireless voice
her attempts to wrong what is
helps me.
I remember
and settle into the folds
comforted by pockets
of my own heat.

Tuning in
to turn off the usual race
my habit is to feel bored
and useless
and I struggle to stay put
breathing into my anxious heart
forcing myself into stillness.

Soon, the nurturing waves
wash over me
with their clear, invigorating light.
I get more still and soft
making sure not to miss one ray
of healing
or one moment of knowing.

Next time I will feel
go to the closet and pull out my shawl
and wrap it around my own shoulders
giving myself the gift
of the slow, heavy, stillness,
sit in its warmth
and welcome the boring waves.

From the heart without fear

Your turn. How can you reframe what you're
making the feeling mean?

An Angel's Aftershave

The love was so big. . .
. . . so new
so full
it crowded out the pain
made me feel a little insane at times
but I recognized
an angel's aftershave
inhaled the scent
eyes closed
a sweet, steady, solid, safe perfume
and knew I was okay
knew I could handle God
washing me out and
hitting the reset button.

I had big things to do, still.

The love was so big. . .
. . . and all I had to do was receive.

From the heart without fear

Your turn. How does it feel to receive?

No Promise of Tomorrow

In my darkest hour
I am the light
On the winds of hope
My heart takes flight

There's no love without fear
No dream without tears
No joy without sorrow
No promise of tomorrow

The blank pages of my life
Are lined with possibility
Every time I take a breath
Gratitude fills the hole in me

In my darkest hour
I am the light
On winds of hope
My heart takes flight

There's no love without fear
No dream without tears
No joy without sorrow
No promise of tomorrow

Each thought in my mind
Every word I choose to speak
Divine purpose planting seeds
Dreams become reality

In my darkest hour
I am the light
On winds of hope
My heart takes flight

There's no love without fear
No dream without tears
No joy without sorrow
No promise of tomorrow

This very moment in time
On the edge of the next exhale
Lies the gift of understanding
The place you cannot fail

Close your believing eyes
Feel it in your core
Love runs through your veins
It's why you were born

Bask in love today
Embrace the face of God
Feel deep into her soul
And know that you are her

In our darkest hour
We are the light
On winds of hope
Our hearts take flight

There's no love without fear
No dreams without tears
No joy without sorrow
No promise of tomorrow

No promise of tomorrow

No promise of tomorrow

No promise of tomorrow

From the heart without fear

Your turn. What do you need to do *today?*

Change

I'm empty inside
hard to be with myself
feeling desperate for love
can't fill the void
left by I don't know what
I don't know how
I don't know why

I'm empty inside
hard to feel the stuff
feeling crazy for something
I can't get
don't know what
don't know what I want
don't know who I am

I'm empty inside
painful in the silence
too anxious for something else
can't be here now
don't know how to be
don't know how to see
can't get a grip on me

Empty inside
want to hide
from the shame
can't make it go away
it's making me insane
making me try too hard
making me cry again

Feeling empty inside
so far away from joy
aching for more
for what I'm not sure
can't soothe this place
can't make the space
to breathe

Breathing into that space
breathing into that place
breathing life into me
breathing me back into being
I can feel the pain
and not fade away
I can feel again if I breathe.

It's all I have
I'll make this work somehow
surrender to pain
surrender and know I'll be saved
surrender all day
let go and exhale
love empty until I feel change

From the heart without fear

Your turn. Can you love 'empty'?

Drawing Lines

I watch planes draw lines in the crisp, blue sky
over a beautiful orange sunrise.
Why can't I draw any of those to save my life?

I'm not high enough for the sky.
And there's no sand at my feet.
But today, I refuse to admit defeat.

My lines sit inside
huddling around my heart
creating a mosh pit to the music of life.

Getting louder, they start to scream:
"Let me out."
"Show me to the world."
"Save yourself, girl!"

And everything I was taught
gets in the way
like bouncers.

"They'll think you're a bitch."
"They won't love you anymore."
"You'll be all alone."

Final message?
"You don't belong here. You're not on the list."
"Take your lines and beat it, sis."

If I can't draw my lines
find the space reserved for my soul
protect her heart and show up full-on. . .

. . . then how will I navigate this bumpy road?
How will I keep love as my goal
if I can't first love myself?

Even if drawing them hurts,
I know what I must do.
Those lines are the healing—for me, and maybe you.

From the heart without fear

Your turn. What lines do you need to draw?

Sandcastles

You're 50, I thought.
What do you want for the rest of your life? I asked.
I'd love to be loved fully,
to be the object of his desire,
to know he sees the sunrise in me
to create bigger love together.

So you must do that for yourself first, I thought.

And she said,
Okay, but I could spend forever doing that.
And? I thought.

And what's the fun in being alone
when the world is one gigantic playground of souls
waiting for you to ask them to meet you in the sandbox?

And someone piped up,
It's more about the power you wield
when you're detached from the need.

So just be love.
Be the object of your own desire.
Trust you're enough.
Pursue joy. . .alone if you must
Put your hands in the sand.

Because when he spies
the sandcastle you've made
he won't be able to help but come around
a little closer to see.

And you can say, "I built this!"
"Isn't it grand?"
There's room for two!"
"Wanna play?"

From the heart without fear

Your turn. What do you need to give to yourself first?

What I Hold Inside

Sometimes what I hold inside is so big
I feel I can't contain it.
I wonder if it's real, true, worthy.
Am I just a fraud,
more wanting than pure
unsure
lost?

Sometimes what moves me is so small
I feel I can't explain it.
I wander in magic, miracle, essence.
Maybe nothing's real,
made up, illusion
delusion
trick.

Sometimes what pains me is so loud
I feel I can't stand it.
I wonder about it's meaning.
Is it random
suffering, hectic
expected
resigned?

Sometimes my soul speaks so softly
I feel I can't translate it.
I wonder about dreams, passion, longing.
Should I share gifts
that sit inside
ride
speak?

Sometimes silence is an ache
I feel I can't tolerate.
I wonder if it's wrapped, a tight mistake.
Why aren't I content
with life
nice
easy?

What I hold inside is so big
I feel I can't deny it.
I know it's true, real, worthy.
I am meant to be
every bit, hair and idea
matter
shine.

From the heart without fear

Your turn. What do you hold inside?

Waiting for Words

A flow of brave words
helps some days
My way of feeling connected
to that bigger thing
beyond my small self
that can handle anything
even killing babies.

The sadness, disgust
and disbelief
form a shield
thicker than any of my life.
Please, brave words
I'm ready to be broken open.

The space remains silent
fuzzy
numb
helpless
afraid.

I think of *my* babies
now young adults
navigating a world
that's repeating old unconscious patterns
and wonder what will become
of their babies.

Will they decide
their world is no place
to try
and let their bloodline
die with them?

I get it.

And while I want
to turn this poem around
and speak about love
it's hard.

This moment
small gratitudes will have to do
hugs, where I can get them
and this message to all of you:

Brave healers: Don't give up.
No matter how ugly it gets
find the love; connect
and keep on changing the world.

From the heart without fear

Your turn. What's your small gratitude?

The World Turns Grey

Leaves
moss
grass
paint my days green
heart color
all around me
heart color
astounds me
abundance. . .clear as day.

Day is blue
sea
see?
Sapphire oceans
glass treasures
yang to stars yin
rainbow light
iris
fires up my eyes.

The burn turns red-orange
berries
fall
sunset
root chakra
juice
so much food.

Soul food screams purple
always has
amethyst
royalty
hydrangea blossoms
tiny flying fairies
glitter. . .

is gold
citrine
sunrise
a girlfriend's shoes
crayon hues
banana.

Now don't you wanna
really feel
the colors of your life?

It's not black and white.

But when people
decide color
is anything less than a miracle
the whole world turns gray.

From the heart without fear

Your turn. What's does your favorite color taste and smell like?

Within the Thick of My Skin

Within the thick
of my skin
are walls I've practiced
erecting.
Protecting my heart
has become second nature,
the armor a habit
a freaky creation I donned
because I was told I had to.

My real warrior shines
through a thin luminescent gown
an open, soft heart
beneath
beaming out between golden creases
awake to all the sorrow
all the joy
bright
because of the shadow.

Today I test the world
shed my skin
opening
to love and miracles
assuming the worst
will be my best
living in the space of not knowing
lingering there
bare.

It's okay if you don't like
what you see
or hear my call
It was meant for me
and all my soul desires.
I'll be me while you disapprove
wait for the feeling
to move
from my chest to the sky.

All this thick skin
ever did
was weigh me down
make me frown
create doubt and fear
and my dear
you can't keep an eagle
from soaring
high.

I'll get more clear instead
hear the voice
of my warrior goddess
realize fear directs me
write, paint, and dance
until the trance of my bliss
comes to kiss your soul
and lead you
to your own light.

From the heart without fear

Your turn. Do you believe you need a thick skin?

Worth the Next Sunrise

I've been told to just sit with this
before.
Loneliness
in the middle of my chest
gripping hard
on my heart.
So I sit
and I feel
and I think
way too much
instead.

And nothing shifts
and no answers come
and I start to wonder
who it was who told me to sit.
I'm not a dog
after all.
I don't work for treats
or praise
or do I?

I sat with it
like good healers do
what I'm supposed to do
if I want to change the pain.
And hours went by
and a day
and I missed a show
where my friends would've been
to hug me
and let me know
I was okay.

I sat forever
waiting
praying
feeling
hoping for something else.
Not a treat
not a pat on the head.
But something to soften
the dread
the regret
the desperate
ache in my chest.

I think,
I should've left
but I was paralyzed
listening to all that.
When instead
I should've been
moving my ass
toward the light.

Not a numbing technique
not a way to escape
not avoiding the pain
but turning my face toward
the sun.

Warming my soul
by the fire of love.
Getting my heart
to a place
it felt held
where it could inhale
again.
Where shadows
are painted pink and orange
with life.

Where no part of me
has to wonder
if I'm worth
the next sunrise.

Yes
next time
I'm moving my ass
toward the light.
Not going to worry
if I'm doing this right.
I'm going to take care
of my own heart
and soul
and trust they know
just how to heal
the pain.

Otherwise
I might waste away
spending so much time
trying to feel again
I forget
there's love
and joy
and light
to be had.
And all I ever really had
to do
was walk over,
grab it gently by the face
hold its gaze
and say
"Hey, I'm here, can we play?"

From the heart without fear

Your turn. What light are you ignoring? Time to go after it.

Woodpeckers on Drainpipes

Early birds start at four
woodpeckers on drain pipes
wait until you've just fallen back asleep
after nights you wondered
if you'd sleep at all,
nights souls ached so hard
they vied for a spot in the record book
of your life
alongside the first heavy summer rain
washing two weeks of pollen
and bad vibes away.

Because you know their sound
you laugh when your bedmate
wakes to the drum alarm and says
"It's a woodpecker on the drain pipe,"
and watch enviously as he falls back asleep
while your heart races along
with the birds,
morning light inspiring thoughts
of coffee and weeks
without ache or yellow-green dust in your lungs.

Cool, fresh rain air floats in on my skin
I'm thinking maybe I should shut the windows
so I can sleep another hour
but the woodpecker moved on
when it heard my voice and
the aching soul in the bedroom next door
is still and breathing slow
and there's another sleep-in morning dream
to be had
before coffee
and problems to solve.

From the heart without fear

Your turn. Early morning or late night—
when do those thoughts move through?

Wounded Gorgeous Girl

Wounded girl
know your worth.
Your desperate cries
only make a deeper hole.
Your wrecked soul
will survive.
You were lovable
the moment we laid eyes on you.
You never had to say a word.
You never had to win.
You never had to try harder.
You never had to be anything else.
Anyone else.
Any better,
or smarter,
or prettier,
or luckier.

Wounded girl
you're a warrior.
Slay your doubt.
Use your fear as fuel.
The cruel words you hear
are coming from you.
Wake up.
Your desperate lies
only feed the wound.
Learn a new way.
Question the day you were taught
to hide,
never asking for what you truly desired,
never owning your truth,
never calling out their bullshit,
never standing up for yourself.

It's time to fill the cracks.
Sturdy the foundation.
Reinforce the launchpad with steel columns
of courage
from which your vision can be heard.
You were meant to heal the world,
wounded girl.
Every goddess has to train.
And you are the master someone's waiting for.
Realize your wound
is the gift
not the curse.
Scars are stronger than perfect skin.
Everything you've ever wanted
lies within the walls you've tried to build
so we wouldn't see the miracle that is you.

Wounded girl
you're perfect just as you are.
A star in the darkness.
Hope in a hopeless world.
The reason we can breathe.
Can't you see?
It's the wound that got you to the place
you can be everything you were meant to be.
The wound
is the freedom you seek.
It holds the key.
It always has.
You were never broken.
The most painful parts
were always the path
to the joy.
Wounded gorgeous girl.
I love you.
It's time to shine.

From the heart without fear

Your turn. How has your wound helped you?

The Seeds of a Poem

Ruby-throated hummingbird
orange and green striped dragonfly
don't tell me these aren't fairies
flying around my face.

They come for the love
the magical space I occupy
they flit around the air
sprinkling fairy dust everywhere.

Buzzing me awake
I can't help but stare
anchored there, amazed
their gaze fills me with questions.

What gift do you bring?
What message do you send?
I'm listening
What magic are you intending?

I feel them linger here
in my heart
long after they depart
leaving tiny glowing embers in my soul.

The seeds of a poem
take root in purple dust
I sit and trust the words
to spill out and do my fairies justice.

Poet's note: Since writing this poem, and many others, about hummingbirds, I was honored to hear the legend of the hummingbird from Jorge Luis Delgado on the tour bus during our author's adventure in Peru in August of 2024. You can read that full story in his book, *Inka Wisdom.* The summary? The hummingbird appears to remind you that all the answers are within, and when you don't have the question anymore, you are a master.

From the heart without fear

Your turn. What part of nature inspires you the most?
What shows up for you?

You Can

One warm, golden-pink beam
pierces through spaces
between the remaining leaves
of ancient trees.
Sacred spaces
where the light shining through
reminds you
there's more to this world
than hate and fear.

Let your gaze steady there.
Take a portrait shot
letting everything else blur
for a moment.
Your heart beats sure
and loud
proud to sit open and reaching
widening the circle
of love.

This practice is everything.
The dream-maker.
The master manifestor.
The salve of all wounds.
The way; the how.
The reason
you have a choice
in the darkness.

Sit here with me
in the still, silent haven.
Build your nest.

Be diligent about resting.
Surrender into
each feeling with curiosity
and a deep, pelvic bowl breath.
Relax.
Inspiration is right here.

Stay a little longer
than you're comfortable.
Wait for what you know
to show itself.
It arrives unexpectedly
as the golden-pink
turns into an orange glow
popping sparks of purpose
as you stoke.

Stir and shake
the old conditioned flakes
of doubt, fear, and hate
—yours or ours—
and blend them into
this pot of soul.
Watch as the love melts
around it all
and something new takes shape.

You are the master chef
at this table today.
You are the teacher,
the guru, and the student,
learning in every moment.
Your creative beginner's mind
finding time to be
without any hints
of wanting or wishing it different.

Lean into the spaces within,
traces of sorrow,
anxious squeezes
pressing on your heart.
Release the bracing.
Recognize who you are.
Repeat a trillion times over
if you must.
Because this might just change everything.

You can change the world.

From the heart without fear

Your turn. What's your "I can" mantra?

The Most Important Thing

The most important thing in my life?

Waking to love, in every possible way
that helps me feel fiercely alive.
My ability to take that inspiration,
available at any moment,
even the impossible ones.

Being awake enough to choose love,
no matter what,
no matter where,
no matter who,
no matter how difficult,
no matter how ripped-open it leaves me. . .
. . . this is the most important thing.

To look at another with complete acceptance,
understanding,
and compassion.
No matter what they've said
or what they've done.
To forgive and move into love
letting that energy be what
infiltrates my heart.

I always have a choice,
so I must attempt to choose love,
not out of duty or obligation
to my parents or teachers
but to my soul.
A promise to take radical, complete care of myself. . .
. . . the same self who'll then
and only then,
have the other-worldly capacity
to give what's necessary to make a change.

The most important thing in my life
is a wild, crazy, big-ass, unexplainable love,
an unfiltered, out-of-the-box, bigger version
than I was originally taught,
a flavor created by me,
tasted only by those who dare
and delighted in by those
courageous enough
to step into another level of vibration
without truly knowing what's in store,
willing to risk it all,
willing to come crashing down,
and rise back up,
dripping in the sacred bath of the full moon
and ready to take on the world.

The most important thing in my life
is the warrior love
I was born to be.

From the heart without fear

Your turn. What's the most important thing for you right now?

Permission

I wait for permission
to live my life
as I see fit
like it's someone else's decision.

I sit quietly
in the corner
waiting
for someone else's right way.

I move about
not realizing
my worth
or the importance of my expression.

In a flash
of enlightenment
I know the truth
which is me.

The me as good as you
the life I choose,
the love
I want to be.

I don't ask
for permission.
This defining moment
sets me free.

From the heart without fear

Your turn. What have you been waiting for permission for?

Reclamation

It was an up-leveling of a different kind,
so intense I didn't recognize the signs.

The Universe always taught me the flow
spelled out what I needed to know:
the way it feels to transform
how it takes what is
and turns it into your dreams
and the life you were born to lead.

But I forgot.

Maybe. . .
. . . just maybe I prayed for it to happen this way
asked God to unlock the gate
so I could run free.
And she gave me exactly what I needed
to create everything.

It all came at once
a gift of chaos and pain
no explanation
only an answer to a prayer for my best life to arrive.
And suddenly what I truly thought I wanted. . .
. . . that well went dry.
I found myself at the bottom of a pit
so deep and dark
I didn't recognize me—again.

Damn, you did it again!

When will I learn?

You stole my identity
forced me to see a bigger, better me
the me who's actually meant
to do that dream I dreamt
once upon a time.

I thought I was her again and again.
Now I realize I had some expansion
to take on.
If I really wanted all that
I'd have to accept the fact
that there was more work to do
more fear to alchemize into fuel
a grander-sized heart and soul to grow
a more masterful circle to curate.

At this rate?
Baby, I'll be there in no time.
In fact, I've arrived today
in the reclamation of my voice
my worth
my dream
my chaos
my pain
my moment of waking
to the depth of WTF-ness
in my circumstance.

I laughed when I saw.
How could I have missed. . .
. . . everything carefully placed on the table
in front of my face
clear as day?
1. Express your love and detach
2. Set your boundaries and cast your line from there
3. Let down your hair and surrender to the sweet spot
of letting go

4. Remember you aren't supposed to know the how;
It's always a surprise and delight

The Universe's fireworks show for your soul
is not a set holiday
or size
or color
or model or make.
It's always the awe and the joy
always the feeling of yes
of ease
of love expressed
always takes care of itself
and lets itself be known

Your doubt, fear, and clench
just brace around the clarity
you spend months blocking yourself from.
If you take off the brakes and break
so be it.
If you break
and everything comes crashing down
don't you get the Divine purpose in that soul-fall
and the power that has your back?

Aren't you ready to receive the support
you always thought you lacked?
Can't you see YOU are what's holding you back?

If the stuck spot feels bigger or harder this time
it's only because you thought holding on tighter
would be the only way to survive.
Instead, that old tactic
created cement inside
and weighed you down so hard
you struggled to rise.

So dreamer, warrior, world-changer, lover. . .
. . . let go.
Break the rules.
Let the old ways die.
Birth something new.
Don't over-analyze the mess.
Confess to the blankness.
Embrace and sit in the middle of it all.
Call the angels to your side.
Reclaim what's yours.
Fly.

What's in store will happily, easily flow
like a cosmic lazer light show
showing the way to the next dance step. . .
. . . as soon as you're ready.

And girl, I know you're ready to dance.

From the heart without fear

Your turn. What will you reclaim for yourself today?

The Harder Work of Love

It would be radical
to offer love to someone who hurt you
or hurt someone precious to you.

To practice love in the face of hate,
socially acceptable hate,
hate there's an excuse for,
is brave.

Even if the part of you
that could feel love
in that instance
is minuscule,
or barely perceptible,
it's worth reaching for.

When you love
in the face of hate
despite what anyone else thinks,
even the person who counts on you
to hate with them,
you've lived life's (and love's) purpose.

It must be why
we're given so many lifetimes
because loving in the face of hate
means you're outcast
until the world catches up.

Hating is easy.
Time to do the much harder work
of love.

From the heart without fear

Your turn. Do you have any love to give?

Smiling to the Sky

So much between
now and then
my mind swirls in
contemplation of
the what ifs and hows
and possible scenarios.

So many moments between
now and that future scene
my mind clogs up with
what might be
how to control
who I should be.

So much flow from
now to who knows
my mind is tired
I want to slow down
and enjoy
the show.

All that noise in my head
my mind filling up
with dread
is just something I do
instead
of being still.

My now provides
everything I desire
if only I can aspire
to stay there
a while
and breathe.

I will hear my voice
ranting again
but notice and stand
in my now.
Free and easy, fiercely alive
in my power.

Smiling to the sky
no need for why
or how or if
loving the drift
of the tide
of my life.

I lay back in it
losing myself
in bliss
knowing
I was meant
for this ride.

From the heart without fear

Your turn. What happens when you get still?

Say It Out Loud

Before they vibrate
from my mouth,
the words are just thoughts
into symbols,
smushed together into sentences,
wished into meanings,
with hope for healing.

I speak them out loud
from a place deep inside
and they are sounds,
melted into rhythm,
connected with tones,
wished into a song or story,
with a hope for connection.

When they are spoken out loud
I step into my power and passion.
I "feel speak" them out
and they are alive,
wished into memories
with hope of a lingering touch
on your heart.

Feel it out loud
for others who can't.
Spread your wings
for those who can't fly.
Just by trying
you will succeed
in helping.

Say it out loud
and find your voice
from the heart
to the tongue
you will speak
the language of spirit
and there will be healing.

From the heart without fear

Your turn. What do you need to say out loud?

Say Yes to Your Soul

Feel the deep ache
now hear the call
everything's at stake
you can't play small

Your life's on the line
your soul's in pain
you know it's time
to make a big change

Say yes to your soul
say yes to yourself
Love is the goal
there is nothing else

It's okay to be scared
the path will unfold
you're more than prepared
It's okay not to know

Feel it all now
don't expect it'll be hard
don't judge the how
take down your guard

Your soft is your power
it's not what they said
you'll thrive every hour
your soul's your best friend

Say yes with your mind
say yes with your body
say yes all the time
with this soul-type karate

Every move you make
that's a yes inside
will soothe the ache
and create a magical ride

When fear comes around
to keep you from shining
put your hands up and shout
and keep fucking riding.

You're not alone tonight
grab a hand when you're scared
You don't need to hide
there's someone who cares

We'll say yes to our souls
to that we'll be true
it starts with being bold
being fearlessly you.

That ache is the way
you know you're alive
stay awake every day
be grateful you've arrived.

From the heart without fear

Your turn. What do you want to say yes to today?

Scribe of God

Step out of the way
your soul needs a running start
for the cannonball into vulnerable truth
she's ready to impart on the world.

Stop worrying whether they'll like it or not,
like you or not.
That knot you're tying
blocking up your throat?
Spoken words sit waiting,
backing up against the clog of not-enough
and soon your pipes will need something more than courage
to regain your flow.

You know they don't sell that kind of Drano.
The kind for "Can't-say-no" so thick
it's rusted out your containment system,
leaking behind the walls,
Invisible. Moldy.
20 years of resentment and fear persists
and one day you'll wake up
and your house is falling down around you
They find you sitting cross-legged
on the floor in the corner
Mumbling "I didn't know."
But you knew.

There is a part of you who always knew.
Who squeezed words out through
tiny crevices where the shame was eating through
Gorgeous words of hope
edged with silvery glitter
Shaped like stars
once in a while they seep through from your heart.
And what do you do?
Wonder if anyone will notice.

Oh no, Scribe of God,
listen to your heart song.
The lyrics may feel too real to appeal to the masses
only you don't know
that song is secretly everyone's. And past the mask
they wear to cover up the pain
the truth sits again, waiting, patiently
for you to fine tune the courage dial
so instead of wanting to die you'll want to see more,
sing more
scribble your delights
to the light of the moon, more.

Know that the fight you feel
between your chest
and your gut,
gutting your insides until
they spill out
for all to smell
afraid you'll wreak of freak
is really who you were meant to be.

She's finally shining so bright
she's come undone
straight into
the joy beam she spent
all those years hiding from.

Scribe of God
pick up your pen.
Pick up your pen again.
Gently guide us deeper in
so we can release
the straight jacket around our inhale.
Pop that buckle open
That jail lacks a deep inspiration.
Bars built with habitual self-doubt
always shouting lies, lying with your worth
after countless late night booty calls

wrecking any shred of what's left
in the name of feeling loved by someone other than yourself.
Holy duck
you know you have the key to the cell,
right?

Scribe?
Are you listening?
You hold it so tightly in your grip.
Your knuckles bleed red
you've read the rules a thousand times
and still insist on thinking that thinking your way through
instead of letting the ink sink in in the lines of rhyme is fine enough.
Instead of stripping the tethers around the wrists of your heart
so they can reach out and feel.

Loosen the grip
Sip from the cup of love
Trust
And if you must doubt, let that be about
whether your words will change you
or the world that day.
Because either way the world goes away
with the prize.
Scribe
Of
God
climb back out of the pool,
find your way back to the line
the cannonball is going to be easier
all the rest of the times
step out of the way of your soul
and let her run to the page.
Share your life
like it's the only thing there is left to do.
Let your words fly.

Let your words fly, scribe.

From the heart without fear

Your turn. Write it down. Anything. Let it flow. What matters to you?

A Perfect Fit

You in me
me on you
like a glove
Stretchy jeans
Puzzle pieces
clicking like Legos
sliding into place
so easy
the right key
between my fingers
unlocks
the universe
can't find where the spoon begins
or ends
bends in my body
wrapped in yours
a hot cocoon
sweet sweat
soothing
simple
soul-centering
senses
softness
(sigh)
sitting silently
sexting my two cents
about our melted bodies
how that feels
and how trying
to write words
with that same
click
never quite does the trick
when all I want is
you in me
me on you
mmmmm
perfect
fit.

From the heart without fear

Your turn. Try your hand at a love poem.

A Piece So Deep

Is there a piece of shame
so deep
you're afraid you won't be able
to pry it off your heart?

Do it's barbed edges
cut your flesh
and pierce
when you move?

Has the cage of unworthiness
been there so long
it's rusted
with your tears?

Does your secret
keep you unwilling
to begin
to look for the key?

Is there a knot so tight
and thick like tar
that it sticks
to your soul?

Do it's toxic drips
burn your skin
and spread
when you breathe?

Has the prison of fear
become so ordinary
you don't notice
you're shriveling?

Is your belief
so real
you forget
where you are now?

From the heart without fear

Your turn. When are you getting stuck in a past story?
Notice and write a new one.

Every Day I Have Left

When you see your bucket list is empty
but turn it over
gently shaking
just in case something falls
from a deeper place
you haven't seen
but nothing shakes loose
you've lived your life
full
you chose and continue to choose
joy
there's nothing left
you have to do
before you die
except keep living life
wild
and free
keep writing poems
staying curious
waiting for adventure
seeking love
expressing gratitude
not attaching to anything
that's not vibing high.
What happens then
is more exciting than any list
you could make
you start to take
ordinary moments
and make them
extraordinary miracles
you see the silver sparkle in your friend's hair
and set your GPS there

determined to find your own
sparkle
Places where you find your true tribe
anywhere Southwest flies
end up being better than
exotic flights
little corners in bars
where people come to tell
their truth
let soul hang out
heal their wounds
those corners light up
with neon signs
"come here and be love."
Be warrior love.
I knew long ago
I wasn't afraid to die
made sure I lived my life
in a way that kept me at peace
at the end of each day
in service of brave
compassionate ways
stillness inside
noticing all the miracles
journaling words
to help me survive.
I knew a long while ago
that life wasn't about lists
at all
but about grabbing moments
by the balls
when you had the chance
and dancing until
sunrise.
And so maybe
the last thing
on my list

would be
a sunrise kiss
after a night of love
and poems
and music
and more moments
helping me
empty that bucket
every day I have left.

From the heart without fear

Your turn. Do you have a list?

My Performance

I love the feel
of cool dawn air in my lungs
and the promise of a poem
in a birdsong.

She tip-toes down the hall
and peeks around the corner of my heart
looking to see if the coast is clear.

With no clutter of fear
to navigate
she's free
and dives onto the slip n slide to my soul
head first.

They dance, wriggle, and shake
bump booties
and wait for me to hear the music,
which shivers me awake
with a careful word or two.

Then a smile.

Then a shimmy, disco-style. . .
. . . as lines flow through my pen
pouring out onto the deserted street
waking up the paper at 2 am
again.

It's party time motherfuckers!
Can't you see?
Life is meant to be loved
with everything you have
so get your ass out here
and dance!

I party a little too hard
as notes spill over the sides
onto the second and third pages;
me trying to convince my neighbors
not to be a grumpy pants
and come and dance too.

But not everyone hears the music.

It's not our job to tune their dial.

It's our job to enjoy
what our own souls do
with the beat of that cosmic bass.
Understand the rhythm inside our own space first,
completely.
See what moves our hips and pens make
when the spotlight beams through
and we find ourselves in the middle
of the stage
unafraid, for once.

The question is. . . Will you dance?

And never mind everyone else's trance.

Will you dance because you can;
take the bigger risk
that someone else is watching
and might just hear the music too
by hearing it through you?

Oh yes,
I love to feel the promise
of a poem.

My dance.

My performance.

And the gift of the magnificence of life
pumping through my veins, waking the neighbors
again.

I wonder if they'll dance with me this time?

From the heart without fear

Your turn. What's your performance? Use the space to dream.

A Fool for Love

You're a fool
You're brave
You're going to ruin your life
You're going to love your new life
You're hurting people
You're saving yourself
You're going to regret this
This will be the best thing you ever did
You'll never be the same
You'll never be the same
You're stupid
You're finally being smart
You're selfish
You finally love yourself
You're a bad person
You're choosing you
You're a bad mother
You were a woman before you were a mother
Things aren't that bad
I'm suffocating
You should try harder
You've tried so hard you have nothing left
You're an idiot
You're a badass hippie force of warrior love
You're giving up
You're letting go
You're not fighting hard enough
You're finally surrendering
You're not enough without him
You're whole and complete
You can't do this
You can so do this
You're kids will hate you
You're kids will love you

This will be the hardest thing you've ever done
It's about time you did hard things
Your friends will leave
Your real friends will still love you
This is going to suck
This's going to free you
It feels like I'm dying
I finally feel alive
You shouldn't want more
You deserve everything you desire
You're doing this to yourself
You're doing this for yourself
You're a fool
You might be a fool—for love.

From the heart without fear

Your turn. What's some of your inner chatter? Call it out.

Sparkling Trees

Late night
Summer
Still
Thick
No Crickets
Laying back
Gazing high
for fireflies
Yellow-green
Christmas lights
Bright blinking
I'm sinking
into bliss
This moment
Mine
Sublime
Simple
Free
Connected to
the breeze
Sparkling trees
Silence
My mind
Kind
Open
Receiving
Believing
in
Miracles

From the heart without fear

Your turn. Connect with what helps you believe in miracles.

Hope Flickers

Hope flickers in my belly
sparkles
dances
and runs off giggling
begging the chase.

I lurch after her; my habit
running
striving
eyes on the shiny prize
believing the chase.

Defeat anchors me breathless
dark
cloudy
and sits in my chest
threatening to squat.

Surrender whispers here
breezes
lightly
inviting me to float
giving me hope.

From the heart without fear

Your turn. What does hope feel like?

Spirals of Light

I wonder
how many times
I ignored the moon
on my way to the airport,
missed the pink-blue hue
ushering out the night,
passed right by
history's silhouette
on the skyline.

I wonder
how many times
I let
the sun shine alone
and stared
at the glow of my screen
instead
a little dead
to the miracles.

I wonder
what it would take
to shake myself awake
notice the mistake
when I turn my back
to the wind
as it carries the leaves
from the trees
giving them a dance floor.

What would it mean
to really see
fully believe
know the magic of life
that spins
around us
in spirals of light
waiting for us
to look up?

From the heart without fear

Your turn. Where do you see the light?

Shine With Me

Sit with me
in stillness
it's where you'll find the nuggets
In the silvery space of silence
sit there
and expand.

Unwind with me
into the tightness
it's where you will find the key
In the confident space of knowing
Release there
and flow.

Float with me
in that space
it's where you'll find the jewels
In the open space of freedom
float there
and let go.

Breathe with me
into your soul
it's where you'll feel hope
In the sweet space of inspiration
Fill yourself there
and soar.

Drop inside with me
into your core
it's where you'll find love
In the fiery space of heart
dwell there
and ignite.

Shine with me
from your heart
it's where your purpose lies
In the golden space of passion
live there
and thrive.

From the heart without fear

Your turn. How can you shine today?

She Came to Start Me Up

When that first warm breeze
kissed my skin
I sat here thinkin
Spring, please come on in;
I've waited so long
to feel your touch.
"Come around here much?"
I say,
playing, googly-eyed with the stars,
listening to cars
pass by outside.
I look up to see
as the breeze picks up
floating pink blossoms
over my face
and I think,
this is the place
I'm meant to be
feeling bliss!
Gratitude then has its merry way
with my soul
making me know
magic exists.
And the moon?
She was born for me,
and all the wild,
courageous
woman I can be.
I gaze at the stars again,
remember I'm here for this
and not the shit
everyone seems to think
is it.

I'm meant for the magic.
The wonder.
The light.
The dark.
Meant for it all.
So I greet the breeze
with all of me
instead of half-assed.
No doubt in my heart
she came tonight,
passed through
to start me up
and help me write this poem.

From the heart without fear

Your turn. What message is coming from the moon for you?

She's Better Like That

I walk
with a river raging inside me
and she's hungry.
Always
hungry.
I feed her heart
and soul
and peanuts sometimes.
Occasionally I forget
she needs to breathe.
The quiet hours come
and she rages
harder
louder;
more anxious
to carve her path
in the stones of my life.
She rises
with the storms.
She's almost better
like that;
running like a maniac,
spilling over the edges,
keeping up with
a faster pace
of flow.
And when she reaches that place
of calm;
no boulders to impress,
no boundaries to push,
she looks around
curious,
like she's supposed to be carving,
or rushing

or spilling over.
She tries breathing.
She tries on
the calm.
But it just doesn't fit.
She was born the river
and was meant to
run
and rage
and flow like a wild fire
out of control
and magnificent.
She's better like that.

From the heart without fear

Your turn. You have a way about you that you don't need to apologize for. What is it?

You Win

You Feng Shui'd everything. . .
. . . except your body
expecting to open manifesting portals
you stuffed with pizza
nourishing every corner of your home
forgetting the actual temple itself
withering away when the inflammation
made your face disappear in the mirror.

You made sacred corners, crevices, and altars
adorned with amethyst and citrine
while sipping chardonnay.
Placed money trees
where all could see
and prayed over your vision board
waiting for the things
that would surely bring joy
but ignored your leaking gut.

Let's judge gently.
This is a profound opportunity
to wake and stake your claim
on the life you desire.
A call to action
for the movement
your perfect vessel begs for.
A cry to detoxify,
clear a channel for the divine
to work through *you*
instead of your perfectly curated living room.

Here's how, my committed friends:

Spend time within.
Clear your mind.
Practice sacred breath.
Follow the hunger, not the anxious mess.
Feast with your fingers, eyes, and nose,
not only your mouth.
Write it all out
and gaze at your truth for once.
Witness your Self.
Be brave
not a slave to opinions of others.
Be bold
when told what to do—make your own rules.
Find the place
in the center of your heart.
Start peeling off a layer of pain
instead of letting cravings make you numb.
Pour gobs of ginormous love on that little one.

Talk to your future self.
She's already here, by the way.
Bask in her purpose and big-ass vision.
Bathe in joy vibes and gratitude.
Eat that for breakfast.
And instead of remembering at two
that you gotta fuel up
choose healthy sooner.

Knowing is Step 1.
Staying true to who you were born to be
is all the rest.
Food, sleep, water, breath. . .
. . . add big love—you'll pass this test.

Fill with what you need to thrive.
Clear, clean, and curate your nest
but don't forget
your beautiful body

is the most important guest
you'll ever be honored to host.
Treat her with respect
dignity
compassion
care
and lastly, some warrior love badassery.

Feng Shui that soul basket, first.
Every thought, bite, belief, and choice
is sacred medicine.
You get to decide how you respond
to this ride.
Hands up
or gripping tight?
Heart open
or armored for the fight?
How will you choose to use
your magical abilities?
Feel it all,
or stuff another Oreo in?
There's no shame, blame, or guilt.
Only choice.
Only power.
Only being a divine channel for the Universe
to play her world-changing game.

You win, goddess.

You win.

From the heart without fear

Your turn. What's one step you can take for your body temple today?

Sunrise

Sunrise holds a promise
hers alone
Only the first light of day
can make you believe
in something new
Her soft, spectacular hues
and early morning mist
cast different shadows
of hope
peace
calm
and you'll breathe into that with all your might
as it washes away yesterday's blues
and helps you
be brave
and begin again.

From the heart without fear

Your turn. What helps you be brave?

The Vibration of Love

from the sacred moonlit night
she rose
from the soft pink sunrise
she rose
from the warm, rugged earth
she rose
from her soul's flaming essence
she rose
and ignited a revolution
brave
worthy
out loud
purposeful
positive
generous
and aware. . .
she rose, lit from within
shining out
feeling everything
healing everything
living the joy
honoring the pain
touching stillness
allowing the vibration
of love
to rule.

From the heart without fear

One Last Life Line

You're only ever one breath away from different energy. That shift can save your life.

Take a quick peek in the mirror. Repeat after me: "I love you!"

With Warrior Love,

Laura

Notes

Notes

Notes

_____
_____
_____
_____
_____
_____
_____
_____
_____
_____
_____
_____
_____
_____
_____
_____
_____
_____
_____
_____
_____
_____
_____

Notes

Notes

Laura Di Franco is the CEO of Brave Healer Productions, an award-winning publisher for holistic health, wellness, and business professionals. She has 30 years of expertise as a holistic physical therapist, 14 years of training in the martial arts, and is the author of 14 books and the lead author of 11 collaborations so far.

More than an inspirational speaker and spoken word poet, Laura's authentic leadership ignites the soul and helps you move through your purpose-driven fears, become a published author, and share your work with the world in a much bigger way.

Laura's writing is inspired by the sunrise, mind-body-soul connection, dark chocolate, and her Jack Russell Leo. She's blissed out most during long walks in the woods or collecting shells on the beach. Before dawn is her favorite time of day.

Writing, publishing, and sharing brave words that build your business is a world-changing healing process we honor and support. Current projects are open for holistic healers, poets, business professionals, and children's story authors who are ready to help us wake the world up to what's possible.

Access the **Brave Healer Resources Vault** for thousands in free resources for author-entrepreneurs: https://lauradifranco.com/resources-vault/

Find more poems in these two places:
To read: https://www.facebook.com/warriorlove
To listen: https://www.youtube.com/channel/UCg8800rajBfvnblw-lc3vtA

Connect with Laura:

Website: https:/BraveHealer.com

Facebook: https://Facebook.com/BraveHealerbyLaura

Instagram: https://Instagram.com/BraveHealerProductions

LinkedIn: https://www.linkedin.com/in/laura-di-franco-1b037a5/

YouTube: https://www.youtube.com/@bravehealerproductions2444

BRAVE HEALER
PUBLISHING

experience what's possible

Opportunities For Poets

The Warrior Love Poetry Page

You can **submit your poem** for a shout-out on our **Warrior Love Poetry Page** on Facebook. Please email that submission in the body of your email to support@lauradifranco.com with:

1. Poem title
2. Poem
3. Signature/title
4. 50-word bio with one link
5. Photograph that accompanies the poem (please include photo credit line).

If approved, your poem will be posted on the page and you'll receive an email with that link. If you don't hear from us within 72 hours, please follow up!

Please make sure to like/follow the page before you submit your poem!

Go here to do that: https://www.facebook.com/warriorlove

Positively Purposeful Poetry YouTube Podcast

Do you have a poetry book you're promoting? Come **be interviewed** by Laura and have the opportunity to read your poetry for a larger audience. Please email us at support@lauradifranco.com with interest.

Make sure to subscribe to the YouTube channel before you inquire.

Go here to do that:
https://www.youtube.com/@positivelypurposefulpoetry8316

100 Poems & Possibilities for Healing Collaborative Poetry Book

Are you ready to join a global community of poets and authors and be published in our next bestselling, business-building collaboration? You'll find more info about all of our active book collaboration opportunities here: https://lauradifranco.com/expert-book-collaborations/

Or feel free to reach out by email: support@LauraDiFranco.com

Brave Healer Productions is proud to be partnering with CopeNotes.com.

Cope Notes uses daily text messages to improve mental and emotional health for organizations, families, youth, and adults in nearly 100 countries around the world. Each anonymous, randomly-timed message proactively interrupts negative thought patterns with psychology facts, journaling prompts, and exercises that are proven to reduce stress, anxiety, and depression by training the brain to think healthier thoughts. Learn more and try it for free at copenotes.com. If you decide to buy a subscription, you can use the discount code BRAVE to score 10% off through our exclusive partnership with Cope Notes!

Resources

National Institute of Mental Health http://www.nimh.nih.gov

American Foundation for Suicide Prevention www.afsp.org

Mental Health America (MHA)
https://mhanational.org/

- **What they offer:** Mental health screenings, educational resources, peer support, and community tools.

- **Who they serve:** Everyone, with a focus on prevention and early intervention.

National Alliance on Mental Illness (NAMI)
https://www.nami.org/

- **What they offer:** Free support groups, education programs, advocacy, and a HelpLine.

- **Helpline:** 1-800-950-NAMI (6264) or text "HELPLINE" to 62640

Crisis Text Line
https://www.crisistextline.org/

- **What they offer:** Free, 24/7 emotional support via text with trained crisis counselors.

- **Text:** HOME to 741741

988 Suicide & Crisis Lifeline

- **Call or Text:** 988

- **Website:** 988lifeline.org

- **What it is:** Free, 24/7 emotional support for people in suicidal crisis or emotional distress.

Crisis Text Line

- **Text:** HOME to 741741

- **Website:** crisistextline.org

- **What it is:** Text-based support from trained crisis counselors, available 24/7.

SAMHSA National Helpline

- **Call:** 1-800-662-HELP (4357)

- **Website:** samhsa.gov/find-help/national-helpline

- **What it is:** 24/7 help for mental health and substance use issues. Offers referrals and information in English and Spanish.

NAMI HelpLine

- **Call:** 1-800-950-NAMI (6264)

- **Text:** "HELPLINE" to 62640

- **Website:** nami.org/help

- **What it is:** Support and information on mental health conditions, treatment, and community resources.

Thank you to our sponsor, Maria Winters, LCPC, who provided this resource list.

Maria is a licensed mental health therapist based in Maryland with over 20 years of experience supporting individuals through life's most difficult moments. Her expertise spans suicide prevention, crisis response, and guiding others through the healing process of rebuilding self-esteem, self-love, and self-worth.

In addition to her clinical work in hospital, emergency, and intensive treatment settings, Maria is a public speaker and wellness educator. Through her website www.thecoachingtherapist.com, she offers free downloadable guides on how to have supportive conversations, build emotional resilience and other topics.

Maria regularly leads virtual and in-person workshops designed to help individuals reconnect with themselves, nurture their mental and emotional health, and cultivate inner strength. Her work is rooted in hope, healing, and the belief that wellness is possible for all.

Instagram: coaching_therapist

Podcast: Wellness Rebranded

Email: mwinters@thecoachingtherapist.com

From the heart without fear

Poetry Heals

What if that thing you're still a little afraid to share is exactly the thing someone is waiting to read to change (or even save) their life?

It's time to be brave.

With Warrior Love,
Laura

BraveHealer.com